Bookworms

Nature's Formations

How Are Canyons Formed?

B.J. Best

Cavendish Square
New York

Published in 2018 by Cavendish Square Publishing, LLC
243 5th Avenue, Suite 136, New York, NY 10016

First Edition

Website: cavendishsq.com

CPSIA Compliance Information: Batch #CS17CSQ

Library of Congress Cataloging-in-Publication Data

Names: Best, B.J.
Title: How are canyons formed? / B.J. Best.
Description: New York : Cavendish Square Publishing, 2018. | Series: Nature's formations | Includes index.
Identifiers: ISBN 9781502628886 (pbk.) | ISBN 9781502628862 (library bound) | ISBN 9781502628893 (6 pack) | ISBN 9781502628879 (ebook)
Subjects: LCSH: Canyons--Juvenile literature.
Classification: LCC GB562. B47 2018 | DDC 551.44'2--dc23

Editorial Director: David McNamara
Copy Editor: Nathan Heidelberger
Associate Art Director: Amy Greenan
Designer: Alan Sliwinski
Production Coordinator: Karol Szymczuk
Photo Research: J8 Media

The photographs in this book are used by permission and through the courtesy of: Cover Galyna Andrushko/Shutterstock.com; p. 5 Rafal Kubiak/Shutterstock.com; p. 7 VK Chernyak/Shutterstock.com; p. 9 Arlene Treiber Waller/Shutterstock.com; p. 11 Steve Johnson/For The Washington Post/Getty Images; p. 13 JTB Photo/UIG/Getty Images; p. 15 Stephen Yelverton Photography/Moment/Getty Images; p. 17 Nature/UIG/Getty Images; p. 19 Scott Prokop/Shutterstock.com; p. 21 Doug Merriam/MCT/Getty Images.

Printed in the United States of America

Contents

Canyons are **valleys**.

They are cut into rock.

They have steep sides.

Most canyons are made
by rivers.

Rivers start in a high place.

They flow to the sea.

Water can **erode** rock.

It wears the rock away.

Some rocks are hard.

Some are softer.

The river erodes softer rock.

The river does not erode hard rock.

This hard rock makes the sides of the canyon.

Rivers make canyons over millions of years.

Sometimes it rains a lot.

There is a lot of water.

This makes a flash **flood**.

Flash floods can cut cracks in rock.

This can make a **slot** canyon.

Slot canyons are narrow.

People hike in canyons.

They think canyons are pretty!

New Words

erode (ee-ROAD) Wear away.

flood (FLUHD) Too much water.

slot (SLOT) A thin hole.

valleys (VA-leez) Low places between two hills.

Index

About the Author

B.J. Best lives in Wisconsin with his wife and son. He has written many other books for children. He has hiked in Canyonlands National Park in Utah.

About BOOKWORMS

Bookworms help independent readers gain reading confidence through high-frequency words, simple sentences, and strong picture/text support. Each book explores a concept that helps children relate what they read to the world they live in.